Literature written for young adults...

by young adults.

Allow yourself to be surprised.

Shadows

Young Writers Chapbook Series

Malachai Moody

Atlanta

Cover design by Kerany Koehl
Editing by Derek Koehl and Tavares Stephens
ISBN: 978-0-9856451-6-8

VerbalEyze Press books are available at special discounts for bulk purchases in the United States by corporations, institutions and other organizations.

For information, address VerbalEyze Press, 1376 Fairbanks Street SW, Atlanta, Georgia 30310.

VerbalEyze does not participate, endorse, or have any authority or responsibility concerning private correspondence between our authors and the public. All mail addressed to authors are forwarded, but the publisher cannot, unless specifically instructed by the author, give out an address or phone number.

VerbalEyze Press
A division of VerbalEyze, Inc.
www.verbaleyze.org

Table of Contents

Shadows

Foreword

Many a black and white speckled notebook has been privy to the growing pains of young artists. They sketch, narrate, poet and rhyme to make sense of the world and orient themselves to the gravitational pull of coming of age. But their musings beg for answers and an empathetic head nod, so YaHeard? Poetics was born.

Whether speaking heartache at the mic, spitting social commentary over tracks or texting observations into the ether, the power and influence of word is undeniable and YaHeard? Poets study the craft, explore their creative process and learn how to promote their artistic endeavors through collaborations with organizations like VerbalEyze, a beacon for young artists.

YaHeard? was founded by Educator-Artists to support the creative stirrings of tweens and teens and the publication of this chapbook honors and encourages the work of a young artists whose passion and talent confirms them as part of a new generation of prolific writers, artists and musicians. Their musings have escaped from first notebooks and into your hands. Answer if you dare; head nod if you must ---this young scribe dares to explore the power of voice.

Ya Heard?

Susan Arauz Barnes
Co-founder, YaHeard? Poetics

Editors' Note

The Young Writers Chapbook Series is an expression of the mission and vision that is core to what we do at VerbalEyze. Through this series, we are able to provide talented, emerging young authors their debut introduction to the reading public. We are grateful that you also share an enthusiasm for young authors and the vibrant and energized perspectives they bring to our shared understanding of the human experience and what it means to live, love, long, lose and wonder as we travel together through this world.

We are pleased to bring to you an exceptional young writer, Regan Nesbit, with this edition of the Young Writers Chapbook. We trust that you will be as engaged and challenged by her words as we have been. Regan is part of an exceptional group of young writers, YaHeard? Poetics. She and her fellow writers are an never-ending encouragement and inspiration to us.

Read, enjoy and, as always, *allow yourself to be surprised*.

Derek Koehl
Tavares Stephens

I Am From

I am from

Arkansas Razorback football

My older cousin telling stories like he's 80

Always talkin' 'bout

"It's a family tradition."

My mom always saying

"We don't have the luxury to do nada."

My other cousin---

Who is technically my cousin

Frying a turkey for the first time

In the front yard

So we don't live in ashes

and

A place of my own at top my closet

Parents

Loving and caring

Their job to keep us safe

Protection, guidance and love

Babies

Innocent young ones

Laughing and playing with heart

In a bigger shadow

Terrible Toddler Reign

I was sitting at the table in the middle of destruction
I have never seen toddlers go so ballistic
They broke the glass table and mirror on my wall

They continue to run around the entire house
Terrorizing me
I'm kind of getting tired of being ignored when I tell them to
stop

But again and again I look away while their mothers whip them
down to earth
I pretend not to see it
I don't listen to them
Instead I play "Call of Duty Black Ops" on PS3

When I open the door to my room, I am mortified
The shock hits me hard, but what can I do
 I just freeze

Tearing through my closet and looking for my books
I can't find my homework or my bag
I clean my room the best that I can and I find them both under

my bed

I speed toward my door
Out for revenge by the time I get done
Would have sent them to infinity and beyond

For some reason I just can't do it
I let them walk
I know I will regret this, but I have to

It's their last day and I can cut them some slack
Now that their terrible toddler reign is over
I think I might miss them

Through the once again quiet house
I sit
At the table

Mind the Gap

In my mind

No education

Is

Like a bullet to the brain

It goes slower

But kills just the same

So

Mind the gap

And

Persevere to greatness

Mind

Don't

Let the haves and have not's

Block your path

Don't let it

Waste your brilliance

Mind the gap

That you cannot jump

Instead

Soar

Fly over

The insurmountable

Mind the gap

And

Make

A cure

For

The poison

That enters the mind

When you don't

Mind the gap

13 Ways of Looking at Entertainment

I.

The rush of competition

That turns to fun

When you're playing at your

Best

II.

sweet

 tangy

 saltines

 entertain

your mouth

III.

Laughing until I can't breathe

Dancing around

We have the time of our

Lives

IV.

Jokes fired like fire crackers

Conversations sparked like fire

29

They laugh and laugh

V.

The excitement rushing from up to down

Unable to stop the yell

The approval

Of the joy that follows

VI.

Experiences

Pain

Advice

All stuck in pages

We read for fun

VII.

Voices

locked in tune

      playing over and over

VIII.

An addiction

Where you can play in the future

While on the couch

IX.

Amusement parks

Getting out of your

Comfort zone for

New kind of fun

At every 50 foot drop

X.

Having it as a

Career is a

Dream come true

XI.

Someone you can

Talk to

And be yourself

XII.

The ideas that flow

With no limitations

And surpass all

Expectation

XIII.

Different than the normal

Exposing the world

That we know little about

A

Airplanes the magnificent

Always speed to

Arrive on time

At

Atlanta's busiest

Airport

Although obstacles

Always block

Amazing

Airplanes that fly

Always

Arrive

Randomness of Yesterday

If we can pick up the slack

Then the future is in the black

If you show respect

You get a tip of my hat

but

Nowadays society's wack

Respect

I see

Respect doesn't get respect

Only in disrespect will you find respect

Is it our humanity

To be completely disrespectful to earn

What's considered respect

Does respect come from fear

Or

Is it possible

For your respect to be rewarded with the respect of others

As I ponder these thoughts I watch my theory fall apart

Those who respect and behave

are placed as low priority

And involuntarily

Pushed aside

Is Life to Live

Is life to live life

Or is life to die?

And if one thinks life is to die

I just wonder

Why

I'm just tryin' to figure out the mystery

Which way to go
   to stay on this road

and

Which way will send me a way where I'll never see the light of
   day

So I have to say life is to live

I wouldn't have it any other way

We're Under Attack

We're under attack

We're at war

Fighting up hill

Women and kids

Fighting men

With lighter skin

I want to fight back

But I can't find my brothers

They're on the streets killing each other

Our minds are wasted

Keeping this up

Victory will never be tasted

Our progress was paused

When music exposed our flaws

The emancipation proclamation never freed us at all

Slavery was the cut

But

Society opened the wounds

With hopes of destroying us all

But

We'll never fall

Over the years

My people have seen it all

We're under attack

And we will fight back

 **Malachai Moody** was introduced to writing in his 5th grade language arts class, but didn't start writing until he was in the sixth grade when he studied haiku and other forms of poetry. His "I am from" poem led Malachai to the world of free verse poetry.

Now he is always looking for inspiration to fuel his creativity. Malachai finds inspiration in reading. He has read books from The Harry Potter series by J.K. Rowling to *The Godfather* by Mario Puzo.

Malachai is 12 years old and lives with his mom in College Park, Georgia.

Photo credit: arauzingink

VERBALEYZE
Press

Empowering young writers to say, **"I am my scholarship!"**

Open call for submissions to the *Young Writers Anthology*!

See your work in print!

Become a published writer!

**Earn royalites that can help
you pay for college!s**

VerbalEyze Press is accepting submissions from young adult writers, ages 13 to 22, in any of the following genres:

- poetry
- short story
- songwriting
- playwriting
- graphic novel
- creative non-fiction

For submission details, visit
www.verbaleyze.org

VerbalEyze serves to foster, promote and support the development and professional growth of emerging young writers.

VerbalEyze is a nonprofit organization whose mission is to foster, promote and support the development and professional growth of emerging young writers.

The *Young Writers Anthology* is published as a service of VerbalEyze in furtherance of its goal to provide young writers with access to publishing opportunities that they otherwise would not have.

Fifty percent of the proceeds received from the sale of the *Young Writers Anthology* are paid to the authors in the form of scholarships to help them advance in their post-secondary education.

For more information about VerbalEyze and how you can become involved in its work with young writers, visit www.verbaleyze.org.

CPSIA information can be obtained at www.ICGtesting.com
Printed in the USA
LVOW13s1620200813

348452LV00004BB/161/P